An Exploration of Alchemy

. . .

This Journey Belongs To:

- - - - - - - - - - - - - -

Copyright © 2025 Akiala I

All rights reserved. No part of this publication may be reproduced, distributed, or transmitted in any form or by any means, including photocopying, recording, or other electronic or mechanical methods, without the prior written permission of the publisher, except in the case of brief quotations embodied in critical reviews and certain other noncommercial uses permitted by copyright law. For permission requests, write to the publisher, addressed "Attention: Permissions Coordinator," at the email address below.

"Consciously Create Your Reality Journey: An Exploration of Alchemy"

ISBN: 978-1-7368647-1-5 (Hardcover)

Front Cover Image by Akiala I

Book Design by Akiala I

First Printing Edition 2022
Second Printing Edition 2025

Published by Absoulute Vibe, LLC

info@akialai.com
support@realityisyours.com

www.Akialai.com

www.Realityisyours.com

"Everything in life gets invented at least twice: first in the mind and second in the physical world."

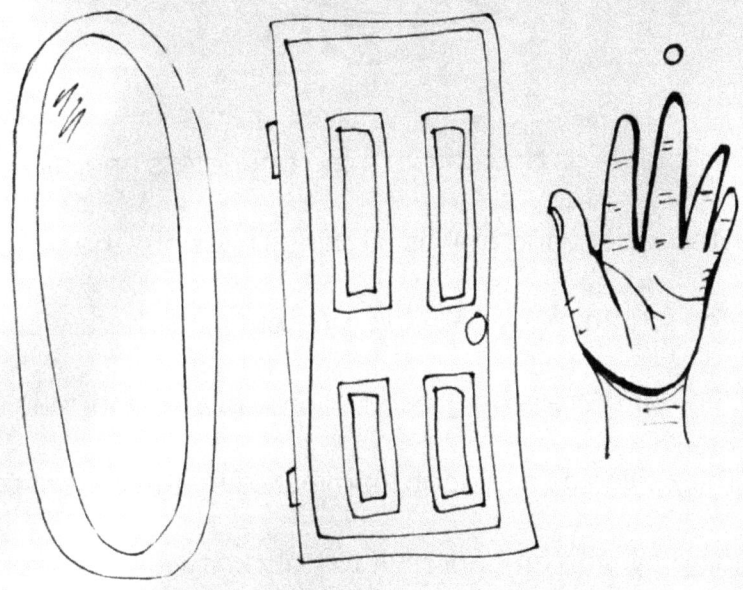

"The decisions you make, and the actions that follow are a reflection of who you are. You cannot hide from yourself."

"Reality is yours."

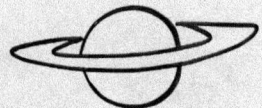

This journey is dedicated to the boundless energy that creates worlds and makes all things possible: the ultimate Creator, whom many call God. Without God, there would be no life, for there is no greater source of creation. May this journey shine as a beacon illuminated by the light of God, guiding all who embark on it to truly know themselves, to love God, and to extend that love to themselves and others.

&

To The Conscious Creators,

You Are Magic.

PSALM 23

The Lord is my shepherd;
I lack nothing.

He makes me lie down in green pastures:
He leads me beside still waters. He restores my soul.

He leads me in the paths of righteousness for his
name's sake.

Though I walk through the valley of the shadow of death, I
will fear no evil: for you are with me; your rod and your staff,
they comfort me.

You prepare a table before me in the presence of my
enemies: you anoint my head with oil; my cup overflows.

Surely goodness and mercy shall follow me all the days of
my life: and I will dwell in the house of the Lord forever.

LETTING GO OF FEAR

You must first let go of what keeps you from reinventing yourself.

THE WHY

What drives you to live & thrive?

PATTERNS

What cycles keep occurring?
It's time for a breakthrough.

EBBS & FLOWS

How do you save yourself?

POLARITY

A whole being must embrace the light and face the shadows.

VIBRATION

How do you keep yourself in tune?

CORRESPONDENCE

How do you influence and interact with your external world?

MENATALISM

You are a Conscious Creator.

HOW TO USE THIS ~~JOURNAL~~:
Journey

1 This journey is designed to be used in order, it is advised not to skip sections & to complete each exercise before continuing.

2 The prompts may require a lot of introspection or bring up intense emotion. Please take your time and be gentle with yourself while moving through your journey.

3 This journal is a safe place to express your thoughts to the fullest. Be fully honest & transparent with yourself. Utilize the extra pages.

4 It is best to not care what others think, in regards to your own journey. Try to remove your own judgements or ego and think from a place of observation & curiosity.

5 This is your journey, get creative, highlight, take notes, change words that don't resonate. Do whatever you need to in order to feel fully present & invested in your transformation.

6 Don't take yourself too seriously. Even though some of the prompts can be serious, the purpose of this journal is to utilize these lessons in order to create your reality and a life of fun, creativity, wholeness and movement.

7 It is best not to suppress any feelings that may arise. If at anytime you feel triggered, please seek a loved one or professional you can process your experience with.

The intention of this journey is to provide a safe chrysalis—a sanctuary for introspection that will catalyze the profound transformation you seek.

This journey is an exploration of self-awareness, alchemy, universal laws, and the first law of thermodynamics: "Energy cannot be created or destroyed, only transformed."

Everything you desire to become or achieve already exists within you.

Our goal is to ease the tension and frequency of resistant thoughts—those that cloud the mind with doubt, scarcity, and fear—while simultaneously aligning with harmonious thoughts that inspire faith, abundance, and confidence.

To engage in this transformative process, it is essential to confront the challenges and suppressed memories that have shaped limiting beliefs and created obstacles to your goals.

Healing is an ongoing journey. Through this journey, you will gain psycho-spiritual tools that can support you for a lifetime. The questions and exercises within this journey are designed to be revisited and applied to future scenarios, offering continual growth and guidance.

Life requires maintenance, and maintenance gives us the gift of choice and free will. What does it mean to "[Consciously] Create Your Reality"?

Each day, each moment, we are making choices. Whether we are aware of them or not, these choices shape our reality. Are there aspects of life beyond our control? Yes. But the mental, spiritual, and energetic capabilities of the human mind are powerful enough to influence our external world and collective experience.

Humans have been gifted the elements—fire, earth, air, water, and ether. When paired with an idea, these elements become the foundation of innovation and evolution. Everything that exists today was once just an idea in the mind of someone who cultivated the will and determination to alchemize the elements and become a Conscious Creator.

Nothing is Impossible

Smartphone / Cell phone (These were all just IDEAS once)
CD
Rocket
Tesla Coil
Light Bulb 24

Are you ready to Consciously Create Your Reality?

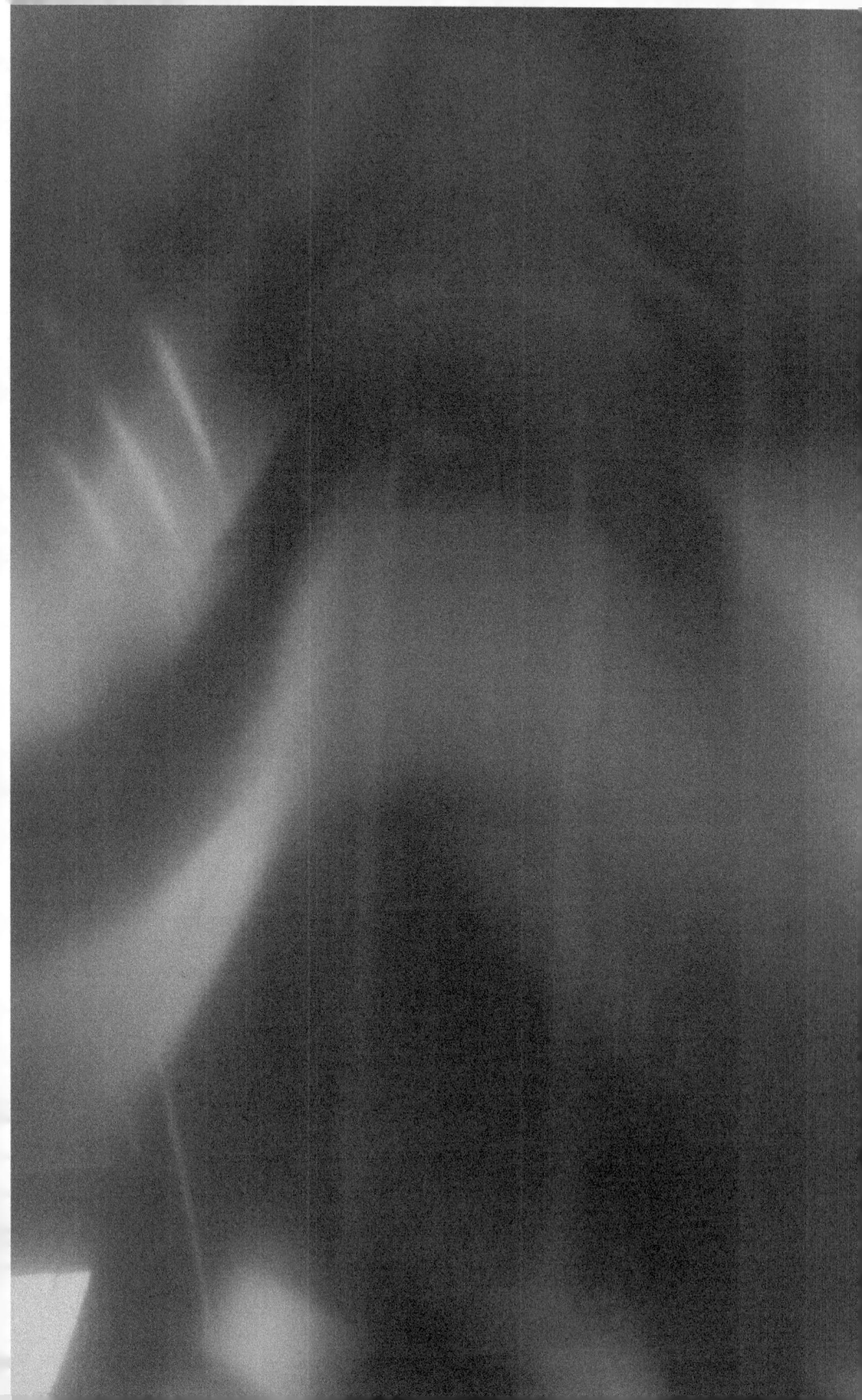

CALENDAR

MONTH:

MONTHLY PLANNER

SUN	MON	TUE	WED	THU	FRI	SAT

TO DO

NOTES

TO-DO LIST

NOTES & DOODLES

MONTH:

MONTHLY PLANNER

SUN	MON	TUE	WED	THU	FRI	SAT

TO DO

NOTES

TO-DO LIST

NOTES & DOODLES

MONTH:

MONTHLY PLANNER

SUN	MON	TUE	WED	THU	FRI	SAT

TO DO

NOTES

TO-DO LIST

NOTES & DOODLES

MONTH:

MONTHLY PLANNER

SUN	MON	TUE	WED	THU	FRI	SAT

TO DO

NOTES

TO-DO LIST

NOTES & DOODLES

MONTH:

MONTHLY PLANNER

SUN	MON	TUE	WED	THU	FRI	SAT

TO DO

NOTES

TO-DO LIST

NOTES & DOODLES

MONTH:

MONTHLY PLANNER

SUN	MON	TUE	WED	THU	FRI	SAT

TO DO

NOTES

TO-DO LIST

NOTES & DOODLES

MONTH:

MONTHLY PLANNER

SUN	MON	TUE	WED	THU	FRI	SAT

TO DO

NOTES

TO-DO LIST

NOTES & DOODLES

MONTH:

MONTHLY PLANNER

SUN	MON	TUE	WED	THU	FRI	SAT

TO DO

NOTES

TO-DO LIST

NOTES & DOODLES

MONTH:

MONTHLY PLANNER

SUN	MON	TUE	WED	THU	FRI	SAT

TO DO

NOTES

TO-DO LIST

NOTES & DOODLES

MONTH:

MONTHLY PLANNER

SUN	MON	TUE	WED	THU	FRI	SAT

TO DO

NOTES

TO-DO LIST

NOTES & DOODLES

MONTH:

MONTHLY PLANNER

SUN	MON	TUE	WED	THU	FRI	SAT

TO DO

NOTES

TO-DO LIST

NOTES & DOODLES

MONTH:

MONTHLY PLANNER

SUN	MON	TUE	WED	THU	FRI	SAT

TO DO

NOTES

TO-DO LIST

NOTES & DOODLES

LETTING GO OF FEAR

Fear

What is fear?

By definition, fear is "an unpleasant emotion caused by the belief that someone or something is dangerous, likely to cause pain, or a threat."

Fear can be a useful instinct, protecting us from potentially harmful situations. However, fear can also become a barrier—one that keeps us from living boldly, truthfully, and authentically.

Many people feel trapped in jobs they dislike, paralyzed by fear of financial scarcity or homelessness. They endure long, draining, and stressful hours, sacrificing their time and well-being for security. While sacrifices can sometimes be necessary, the cost of living in fear—rather than pursuing a life aligned with truth and joy—can be even greater.

Fear, when unchecked, becomes an enemy of evolution. To create meaningful change in our lives and in society, we must be willing to take risks, step into the unknown, and try things we've never done before. Without these bold steps, we risk perpetuating the same draining cycles again and again.

This doesn't mean we should all quit our jobs tomorrow. But if you find yourself constantly unhappy, dreading each new day, it's worth asking: "Am I living in fear?"

Are you willing to be brave, even if it means stumbling a few times, to pursue the life of your dreams?

You've been given this incredible gift: the opportunity to live and create a life that is fulfilling, meaningful, and uniquely your own. Don't let fear hold you back. Don't wait until it's too late.

PROMPT

WHAT ARE YOU AFRAID OF?

Write, list and/or draw the things you are afraid of. For more introspection, write why you are afraid of those things.

/   /

PROMPT
WHAT IS HOLDING YOU BACK?
Write, list and/or draw the obstacles that you believe
limit you from overcoming your fears and doubts.

/   /

EXERCISE
NEW ACTIONS

Now that you have written what's holding you back, write, list and/or draw the actions you can take to overcome those challenges.

EX: If the obstacle is "not enough time for creative projects" a new action could be to "schedule an hour every week for creative time."

NEW ACTIONS

EXERCISE

OLD TAPES | NEW TAPES

On the "Old Tapes" side write down harmful stories you have told yourself. EX: "I am not worthy of love."

On the "New Tape" side write the positive opposite of that story EX: "I am worthy of love."

After listing all of your "tapes" cross out the old tapes and read your new tapes out loud.

OLD TAPES	NEW TAPES
~~I am not worthy of love~~	I am worthy of love

/   /

OLD TAPES	NEW TAPES

/ /

EXERCISE

I AM AFFRIMATION

Write I am statements declaring the admirable characteristics you want to/currently embody.

EX: "I am patient" - "I am becoming more confident everyday" - "I am grateful" - " I am a spiritual being having a human experience" - "I am loved".

Speak your affirmation aloud daily or when you need assurance.

/   /

I AM AFFRIMATION

/   /

CHALLENGE

DO SOMETHING UNCOMFORTABLE

Find a safe but thrilling activity that will allow you to get out of your comfort-zone. Free yourself from the judgement of others. Be brave. It's okay to look/feel silly.

Here are just a few examples of activities:

- KAREOKE

- A DANCE CLASS

- PUBLIC SPEAKING

- PAINTING

- DRESS UP AS YOUR FAVORITE CHARACTER

- TRY A NEW FOOD DISH

- LISTEN TO A NEW GENRE OF MUSIC

- VISIT HISTORICAL OR ODD PLACES- IN YOUR CITY

- ASK YOUR FAMILY/FRIENDS WHAT IS SOMETHING NEW YOU SHOULD TRY

WHAT UNCOMFORTABLE ACTIVITY DID YOU DO?

Write about your experience.

EXTRA PAGES

YOU BEING ALIVE IS A MIRACLE

and • You Affect More
Lives than You Can Possibly
• Imagine •
in The Most Beautiful Way!

95

From "100 Things" By Akiala I ©

THE WHY

When life gets challenging,

what motivates you to keep going?

Your "why" is the reason you wake up each day and strive for a life filled with purpose, passion, and gratitude.

By simply being born, you have forever impacted the universe. Your existence matters. Even if your "why" is simply "to live," that is more than enough. Over time, your "why" may shift and evolve, reflecting the changes in your life and values.

Discovering your "why" is essential. It serves as both a compass to guide you toward a life aligned with your deepest values and a source of strength when you feel lost, sad, or uncertain about your purpose.

Ask yourself:

- Who are the people in your life you are grateful for?
- What moments do you cherish most?
- Do you dream of inspiring others and creating positive change in the world?

In the fast-paced rhythm of life, it's easy to lose sight of the simple joys and take life for granted. We must remind ourselves to slow down and savor the little things:
A hot cup of tea. A sunset. Laughter. The beauty of flowers. The warmth of friends and family.

Every moment is a gift, and we must strive to cherish each one. Because, in truth, none of us know if we will ever have the chance to experience this miracle of life again.

PROMPT

WHAT ARE YOUR GOALS?

Write, list and/or draw your short-term and longterm goals.

/   /

PROMPT

WHAT ARE YOUR INSPIRATIONS?

Write, list and/or draw the people, places
and/or things that bring you joy and hope.

/   /

PROMPT
WHAT DO YOU DO FOR FUN?
Write, list and/or draw the activities that make you feel the most present and alive.

/   /

EXERCISE

DOODLE YOUR FUN SELF

Create a simple or elaborate doodle below of what you look like or what you do when you are having the most fun. It can be as abstract or realistic as you want.

/   /

EXERCISE

YOUR WHY

Write, list and/or draw the reasons you enjoy being alive
and what or who motivates you to keep going in life.

/   /

YOUR WHY

/ /

CHALLENGE

CREATE A VISION BOARD

Compile images that encompass your why, your goals and the things that inspire you and bring you joy. You can make a physical vision board with printed or magazine images or you can make a digital collage using images from the internet. It is advised to put your vision board in a place you will see it daily.

Dream big!

Pinterest and Canva are great online resources for gathering images and creating vision boards.

Here is an example of vision board images:

Description of the vision board elements:

Creativity, loving family, romance, abundance, coastal travel, health, nature.

If you have never made a vision board and don't know where to begin, there are many online examples and video tutorials.

/   /

WHAT ELEMENTS DID YOU PUT ON YOUR VISION BOARD?

Describe your vision board.

EXTRA PAGES

  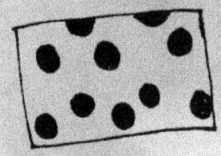

Notice Patterns.

WHEN something keeps occuring there is something for you to realize and learn from that pattern.

From "100 Things" By Akiala I ©

PATTERNS

Patterns

Almost everything we experience in life is an external

reflection of our internal world.

In other words, our thoughts and emotions attract situations

and scenarios that match

their vibration.

Masaru Emoto, author of The Hidden Messages in Water,

conducted fascinating experiments demonstrating how

human consciousness—our thoughts and emotions—can alter

the molecular structure of water.

If we accept his findings as truth, it suggests that human

consciousness has the profound ability to reprogram not only

our own molecular structure but also that of the Earth, given

that both our bodies and our planet are predominantly

made of water.

Consider a recurring life pattern, such as, "Every time I get into a relationship, the same conflicts arise, or it always ends the same way." Often, we blame others, feel victimized, and wonder why the same situation keeps repeating.

Repetitive patterns like these are a signal that it's time to reprogram our thoughts and emotions in order to attract new experiences and outcomes.

Creating healthier patterns begins with your relationship to yourself. How can you expect others to truly love or respect you if you don't love and respect yourself? Likewise, how can you authentically love and respect others if you don't extend that same care to yourself?

The journey to new experiences and meaningful change always starts within.

PROMPT

WHAT DO YOU LOVE ABOUT YOURSELF?

Write, list and/or draw your favorite characteristics.

/   /

PROMPT

WHAT ARE YOUR PATTERNS?

Write, list and/or draw the things that you have
noticed continually occur in your life.
EX: "getting so overwhelmed starting a new project that
I procrastinate." or "I am belittled at jobs."

/   /

EXERCISE

WHEN DID IT START?

Choose a pattern from your list and write, list and/or draw when & how you believe this pattern began. You can repeat this exercise with your other patterns listed.

/   /

WHEN DID IT START?

/   /

CHALLENGE

TAKE YOURSELF ON A DATE

Allow yourself moments to get to know yourself again. Maybe your favorite color or other preferences have changed. Being human means you can evolve and change at various paces. Take yourself on a romantic date (just you!) and get to re-learn yourself as if you were getting to know a stranger.

Here are some self date ideas:

- LUNCH IN A PARK

- AMUSEMENT PARK

- BOTANIC GARDENS

- MUSEUM

- A HIKE/WALK

- COOK A NICE DINNER

- HOME SPA DAY

- PLAY 20 QUESTIONS

- TAKE A WORKSHOP CLASS

- GO TO THE LIBRARY

- RECORD A FAKE OR REAL PODCAST EPISODE

/ /

REFLECTION
HOW WAS YOUR DATE?
Write about your experience.
Did you learn anything new about yourself?

EXTRA PAGES

From "100 Things" By Akiala I ©

EBBS & FLOWS

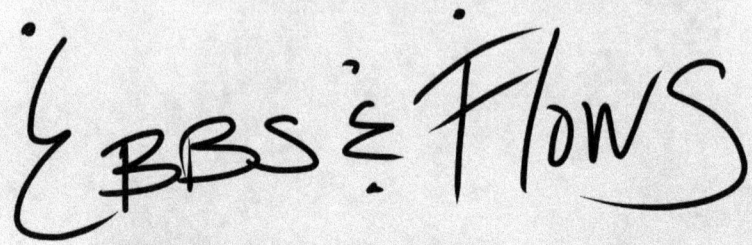

Ebbs & Flows

The "ups" and "downs" of life are inevitable.

How could one truly experience joy without having known sadness? Our ability to feel the full spectrum of emotions is what makes life dynamic, rich, and uniquely human.

In movies, we're drawn to stories of character growth—the trials and tribulations the protagonist faces, the struggle that transforms them. Every human craves their own "Hero's Journey." We romanticize "the struggle" and cheer for the underdog, moved by the alchemy that turns challenges into triumph and characters into heroes.

But in real life, there are moments—sometimes many—when we feel lost, hopeless, lonely, or consumed by sadness.

Feeling sad is okay. Crying is okay. Feeling lost is okay. These emotions are valid and necessary. But when we remain stuck in despair and lose all hope in ourselves, that is not okay. We must never give up on ourselves or our potential for joy.

There are many factors that contribute to unhappiness—diet, environment, relationships, and more. Recognizing these influences is key to understanding how to shift our inner and outer worlds.

In this section, we will explore ways to alchemize your external world and guide yourself back to joy and gratitude during troubling times.

When you feel stagnant or weighed down by sadness, the first and most important question to ask yourself is: "Am I ready to heal?"

Only when you are truly ready can you begin the process of easing yourself back into joy.

PROMPT
WHAT ARE YOUR TRIGGERS?

Write, list and/or draw the things that bring up feelings of fear, scarcity, sadness and/or anger.

PROMPT
HOW DO YOU GET BACK TO JOY?
Write, list and/or draw the things that always cheer you up and help you feel more positive.

/   /

PROMPT

HOW DO YOU HEAL YOURSELF?

Write, list and/or draw the things you do to feel better
spiritually, mentally, emotionally & physically.

/   /

CHALLENGE

MAKE A PLAYLIST

Using your favorite music App or Youtube, make a playlist of music and/or videos that make you dance, sing, think, bring back good memories and relax you.

Here are some music suggestions:

- JOAO GILBERTO

- REMEMBER THE TIME x MICHAEL JACKSON

- ANGEL x LALAH HATHAWAY

- MAMA USED TO SAY x JUNIOR

- SPECIAL STAGE x THUNDERCAT

- MORE x FLYING LOTUS & ANDERSON PAAK

- ERYKAH BADU

- ONE x METALLICA

- LADY X D'ANGELO

- IASOS

- JACOB COLLIER

EXTRA PAGES

Life is All about Perspective

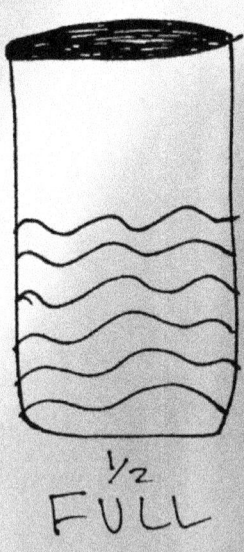

1/2 FULL

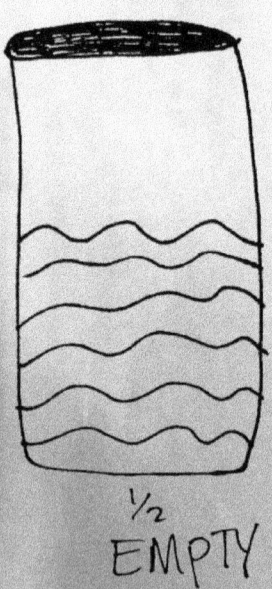

1/2 EMPTY

From "100 Things" By Akiala I ©

POLARITY

Life, as we know it, is duality and polarity.

Day and night. Right and left. Hot and cold. Love and hate. Duality exists in all aspects of life. From a young age, we are often presented with the narrative of good versus bad—a battle where only one side can prevail.

Yet, within every person lies the capacity for both great harm and great healing. We are often taught to suppress the side of ourselves that is animalistic, survival-driven, or capable of causing harm. But denying this "shadow" or "beast" within us disconnects us from nature and from our most authentic selves.

Most people like to think of themselves as inherently good. But consider this: if desperate times called for desperate measures, how would you react? Many would discover that their initial response might not be peaceful or positive.

Understanding your "shadows"—the parts of you that arise in anger, fear, or desperation—is essential to becoming a person who is fully self-aware.

You must learn to embrace and make peace with all aspects of yourself.

The goal is not to suppress or eliminate your shadows. Resistance only strengthens them, ensuring they persist until they can no longer be ignored. Instead, we must confront them intentionally and thoughtfully.

In this section, we will invite our "inner demons" in for a brief visit. We will have a conversation with these aspects of ourselves, seeking to understand why they exist, what fuels them, and how they can be expressed in healthier ways. This is an opportunity to make peace with your darkness—to integrate it into the whole of who you are.

PROMPT
WHAT ARE YOUR SHADOWS?

Write, list and/or draw the qualities of yourself you believe at times can be weaknesses. EX: "I procrastinate a lot" or "I speak negatively about myself and others"

/   /

PROMPT
WHAT ARE YOUR BEST TRAITS?

Write, list and/or draw the qualities of yourself you believe at times can be strengths. EX: "I am considerate of myself and others" or "I am creative"

PROMPT

WHAT ARE HEALTHY WAYS YOU EXPRESS ANGER/SADNESS?

Write, list and/or draw the ways you currently process and release big emotions and come up with new ways of expressing your emotions.

/   /

EXERCISE

WHOLENESS

Create a simple or elaborate doodle below of what you look like or what you do when you are expressing yourself to the fullest.

WHOLENESS

CHALLENGE

WRITE A LETTER & BURN IT

On an extra sheet of paper write a letter fully expressing your true uncensored emotions towards an event you felt like your voice was suppressed. This is a safe space to finally say all the things you would have liked to say in that moment.

Ex: Maybe a friend or family member said or did something that was hurtful but you didn't say anything because you didn't want to argue or didn't feel safe. Think of a memory when you felt unable to share your truth and/or outrage.

After writing the letter you can safely burn or tear it. Here is an example letter, you can also create your own.

Dear _____,

It truly hurt me when you said,"_____"
It brought up feelings of _____.
What you said has still affected me until today. I let your words cause me to _____.

In that moment I wish I could have responded by saying,"_____"
but I didn't say anything because I felt like _____.

I release your words and actions because I am creating a life of empowerment & freedom and will no longer let the past continue to harm my future. Starting today, I will have more courage to speak up for myself and express my truth.

Sincerely, _____

EXTRA PAGES

VIBRATION

Vibration

All of life is vibrating; nothing is truly solid.

When you zoom in small enough, you'll find that what appears solid is actually vast amounts of space filled with atoms, electrons, and other particles—each separated by relatively enormous distances. This truth reveals that we are, at our core, energetic beings. And like fingerprints, every human possesses a unique energetic frequency imprint.

Thoughts, light, color, and sound are all vibrations of energy that can be measured in wavelengths and frequencies. For instance, the color blue has a wavelength of 450-495 nanometers and a frequency of 606-668 THz (terahertz), while red has a longer wavelength of 620-750 nanometers and a lower frequency of 400-484 THz.

Similarly, our thoughts create vibrations.

Different thoughts emit distinct wavelengths, ranging from low to high frequencies. These thought frequencies contribute to our overall energetic frequency imprint and directly influence our experiences, in accordance with the Law of Attraction.

The Law of Attraction is a universal principle stating that like attracts like—energies of similar vibrations naturally gravitate toward each other. Positive thoughts tend to attract positive outcomes, while negative thoughts draw in negative experiences. This principle also explains why people with shared interests or similar vibrations often find themselves drawn to one another.

As energetic and electromagnetic beings, what we focus on and feed with our energy grows. As the saying goes, "What you water grows."

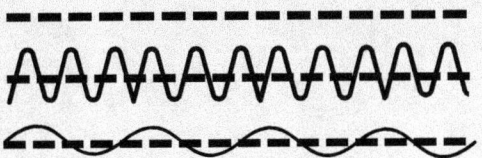

PROMPT

WHAT QUALITIES DO YOU LOOK FOR IN A SOULMATE?

Write list or draw the admirable qualities you would like to and/or currently experience in a romantic partner.

PROMPT
WHAT QUALITIES WOULD YOU LIKE TO EMBODY MORE OF?

For this prompt, let's say that you are your own soulmate.
Do you exhibit those qualities on your previous list?
Which qualities would you like to personify more?

/   /

EXERCISE
QUANTUM CELLULAR REVITALIZATION

This visualization exercise is designed to help you connect with and revitalize your body on a cellular level. It will take 15–30 minutes, so find a quiet, comfortable place where you won't be interrupted. Optionally, you can enhance the experience by playing soothing meditation music.

Step 1: Set the tone.
Before you begin, give yourself permission to become an impartial observer. Release any judgment about the images or sensations that arise, and let go of any expectations of perfection. This is a time to explore freely and without pressure.

Once you are settled and mentally relaxed, close your eyes and imagine placing a single cell from your body in your mind's eye—the space right between your eyebrows.

Step 2: Observe your current cell.
Using your mind's eye like a microscope, explore the cell in detail. Notice its shape, texture, color, smell, and movement. Simply observe it without fear or judgment, even if the images that arise feel unpleasant.

Step 3: Reimagine your cell in its healthiest state.
Now, envision this cell in its most vibrant, healthy, and harmonious form. Let your imagination run free! Your new cell could look like a sparkling gem, a glowing orb, or something more playful—perhaps an octopus, a pizza, or even an octopus-pizza. There are no limits here.

Once you've created this new, revitalized cell, imagine it radiating a glowing, silvery-blue light—or any color that feels right to you.

EXERCISE
QUANTUM CELLULAR REVITALIZATION

Step 4: Transform your body.
Visualize this glowing cell sending out waves of light, transforming every single old cell in your body as the light spreads. Picture the light starting at your mind's eye and flowing slowly down through your entire body, reaching your chest, arms, abdomen, legs, and finally your toes.

Step 5: Radiate outward.
Once every cell in your body has been renewed, imagine this radiant light extending beyond your physical body. Visualize it expanding outward to encompass your home, your community, your continent, and finally the entire world.

You can choose to let this light remain around the world, or gently bring it back into your body, feeling it settle within you as a source of vitality and peace.

Step 6: Reflect and complete.
When you feel the exercise is complete, open your eyes and take a few moments to reflect on the experience. How did it feel? What did you observe? Did anything surprise you?

This practice is a reminder of the power of your mind and imagination in fostering healing and connection, both within yourself and with the world around you.

EXERCISE
QUANTUM CELLULAR REVITALIZATION
Write, list and/or draw the qualities of your old cells.

/   /

EXERCISE
QUANTUM CELLULAR REVITALIZATION

Write, list and/or draw the qualities of your new cells.

CHALLENGE

CLEAN/ORGANIZE SOMETHING

Time for some deep cleaning. Choose an area of your environment that needs some re-organizing and cleaning. Try moving things around to give it a new look.
Put on your music playlist to make it more enjoyable and relaxing.

/   /

EXTRA PAGES

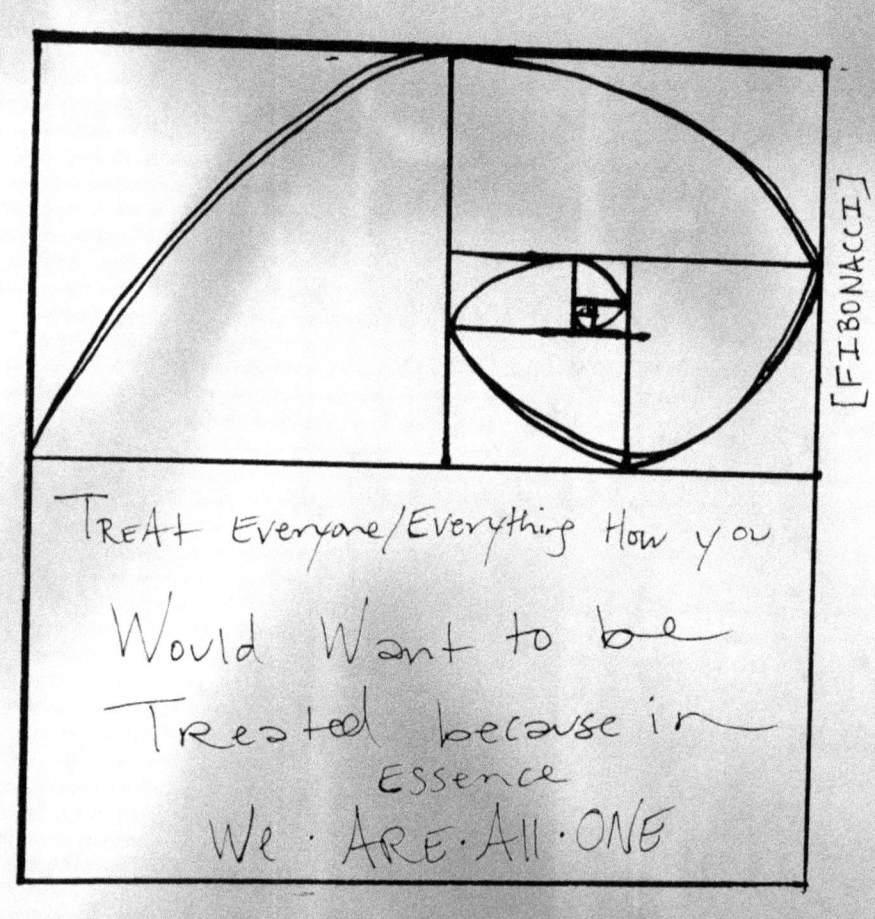

CORRESPONDENCE

Correspondence

We Are the Mirror of Creation

We are made in the image of the Universe, born of the same energy that births worlds and galaxies. Just the act of breathing sends ripples across the vast ocean of existence. In essence, we are the mirror of creation itself.

Recognize the incredible power you hold—and the profound responsibility it carries. It is our sacred duty to heal, to let our light shine brightly, and by doing so, inspire others to shine as well.

As above, so below; as within, so without.
Every thought, action, and intention reverberates not only within us but throughout the entire cosmos. Simply by being born, we have already created vast ripples in the multiverse. Through our choices, we spark butterfly effects of change, shaping our reality and the world around us.

The Earth, too, is a living, breathing organism. It responds to our thoughts and actions, constantly measuring the depth of our consciousness and the purity of our hearts.

Consider the Earth as a garden. When you nurture it—tending to the soil, planting seeds, watering, learning, and caring for it—it flourishes.

But if you poison it and neglect it, it withers and dies. Our minds and souls are no different; they are like gardens. The state of our inner world will always be reflected in the outer world. If we desire true and lasting change in the world, we must first cultivate it within ourselves.

After fostering personal transformation, the next step is to strengthen and improve our relationships with family, community, and the collective.

Watch as the world mirrors the changes you've made within. When you align with love, healing, and care, that energy will ripple outward, transforming not only your own life but also the lives of others and the world as a whole.

PROMPT
HOW ARE YOUR RELATIONSHIPS?

Write, list or draw the state of your relationships with family, friends and acquaintances.
How can you improve your relationships?

/   /

HOW ARE YOUR RELATIONSHIPS?

/   /

PROMPT
HOW IS YOUR HEALTH?

Write, list and/or draw the state of your health and how your body feels.

/   /

PROMPT
HOW WOULD YOU LIKE YOUR HEALTH TO IMPROVE?

Write, list and/or draw things you would like to add or take away in order to improve your overall well-being.

/ /

PROMPT

HOW IS YOUR RELATIONSHIP TO MONEY?

Write, list and/or draw the state of your finances.

/   /

PROMPT

WHAT ARE YOUR FINANCIAL GOALS? WHY?

Write, list or draw what you would like to achieve financially and why.

/   /

CHALLENGE
GO INTO NATURE

Find a scenic hike nearby and spend a few hours in nature. Make sure you are prepared and properly research the area you plan to venture into. If possible find a soft grassy area and place your bare feet on the ground for the benefits of "Earthing." Quiet your mind to be present and immersed in in the scene around you. Write your plan & what you need to bring below.

/   /

/ /

REFLECTION

HOW WAS YOUR NATURE ADVENTURE?

Write about your experience.

EXTRA PAGES

MENTALISM

MENTALISM

"We accept the reality with which we are presented."

– Christof, The Truman Show

Every object, every law, every theory has been innovated or perceived by humans through the senses. Our senses gather information about the world and respond to its stimuli. Without them, our experience of life becomes profoundly limited.

Scientists estimate that humans use only 10% of their brain's capacity. What hidden senses and untapped capabilities lie within the other 90%?

How can we unlock more of our potential?

We can choose to be conscious creators of our reality.
If something doesn't exist that we believe should exist we must "plant the seed" and strive to create it.

Humans have existed for thousands of years without money..

We don't always have to dismantle, burn, protest, ignore or destroy something in order to create the change we desire. To transform, it is required to choose something different.

Choose something that is more in alignment with your truth. Your heart, your brain and your gut will always tell you the truth, if you have the courage to truly listen. The answers you seek are within you and all around you.
Reality is yours to create.

You are magic.

YOU ★ ARE
~~A~~BSOULUTE

MAGIC

AND YOU BETTER

BELIEVE IT!

'98

From "100 Things" By Akiala I ©

- The power of apparently influencing the course of events by using mysterious or supernatural forces.

- Something that has a delightfully unusual quality.

- Very effective in producing results, especially desired ones.

PROMPT

WHEN HAVE YOU MANIFESTED SOMETHING YOU REALLY WANTED?

Describe a time when you had a goal or object that you wanted but didn't necessarily have the means to obtain it. How did you end up accomplishing the goal or obtaining the object?

/   /

MANIFESTATION

EXERCISE:
BE. DO. HAVE.

For this exercise you must free yourself of any and all limitations. If there were no obstacles at all in your life, what would you want to be, do and have?
Write, list and/or draw your answers.

/   /

BE, DO, HAVE

CHALLENGE
CREATE A RELIC

Using craft materials or objects you find around your home, design a unique relic that symbolizes the completion of your "Create Your Reality Journey."
This object can be anything—a small charm, a painted rock, a vision board, or even a jar filled with symbols of your growth and dreams. Its purpose is to serve as a tangible reminder that you are magic and have the power to consciously create and shape your world.
Let your creativity flow, and enjoy the process of bringing your imagination to life.
Sketch your concept below:

/   /

REFLECTION

DESCRIBE YOUR RELIC

Write about your creation.

EXTRA PAGES

You have completed your journey...

Only 2
Begin Again

Welcome to your
new Adventure.

I Am your Witness...

From "100 Things" By Akiala I ©

NOTEBOOK/
SKETCHBOOK

/   /

1 / 1

/   /

/   /

For More Titles & Information

Please Visit:

www.Akialai.com

&

www.Realityisyours.com

www.ingramcontent.com/pod-product-compliance
Lightning Source LLC
Chambersburg PA
CBHW060048230426
43661CB00004B/698